My Body Needs
EXERCISE

by Jenna Lee Gleisner

amicus
high interest

Amicus High Interest is published by Amicus
P.O. Box 1329, Mankato, MN 56002
www.amicuspublishing.us

Library of Congress Cataloging-in-Publication Data
Gleisner, Jenna Lee.
  My body needs exercise / by Jenna Lee Gleisner.
     pages cm. -- (Healthy me!)
  Includes index.
  ISBN 978-1-60753-586-7 (hardcover) -- ISBN 978-1-60753-686-4 (pdf
ebook)
  1. Physical fitness--Health aspects--Juvenile literature. 2. Exercise--
Physiological aspects--Juvenile literature. I. Title.
  RA781.G544 2014
  613.7--dc23
                                2013046273

Photo Credits: Shutterstock Images, cover, 4, 7; iStockphoto, 2, 12; Sergey
Novikov/Shutterstock Images, 8; Red Line Editorial, 11; Monkey Business
Images/Thinkstock, 15; Dragon Images/Shutterstock Images, 16; Tatyana
Vyc/Shutterstock Images, 18–19, 22; Patrick Foto/Shutterstock Images, 20

Produced for Amicus by The Peterson Publishing Company
and Red Line Editorial.

Designer Becky Daum
Printed in the United States of America

10 9 8 7 6 5 4 3 2

TABLE OF CONTENTS

Exercise   4

Be Active   6

How Much?   8

Strong Heart   10

Strong Lungs   12

Strong Bones   14

Strong Muscles   16

Stretching   18

Make Exercise Fun   20

Get Started Today   22

Words to Know   23

Learn More   24

Index   24

EXERCISE

Exercise is activity we do with our bodies. Running is exercise. So is riding your bike. Why do we need to exercise?

BE ACTIVE

Exercise is good for us in many ways. It helps us grow strong. It keeps us healthy. Our bodies can gain extra **weight** if we are not active. This makes it harder for our bodies to work well.

HOW MUCH?

Exercise for at least 60 minutes each day. Playing a computer game is fun. But it is better for your body to move. Go outside and play instead.

STRONG HEART

The heart brings blood to every part of your body. It also brings **oxygen**. Exercise makes your heart work harder. This makes your heart stronger so it can do its job better.

Healthy Hint

Run or jump rope outside. Running and jumping rope are great heart exercises.

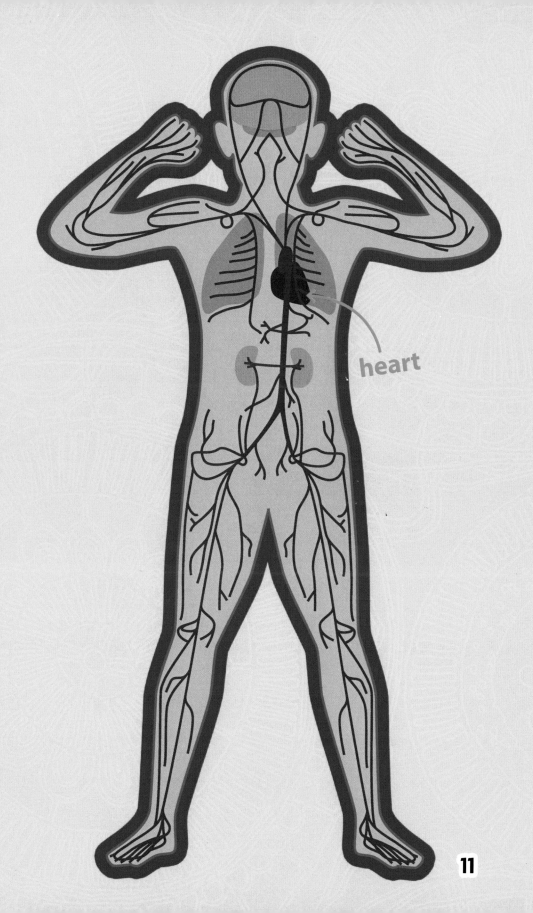

heart

STRONG LUNGS

The body needs oxygen to work. Exercise makes our lungs work hard. We take deeper breaths. The lungs bring in more oxygen from the air. This helps make the lungs stronger.

STRONG BONES

Exercise builds strong bones. We need our bones to stand up. Play and exercise to use your bones. Your bones will grow stronger.

Healthy Hint

Play a sport, such as tennis or soccer. Playing a sport is a fun way to build strong bones.

STRONG MUSCLES

Our **muscles** need exercise, too. Muscles move our bones. Push-ups are a good way to make muscles strong. You can also try pull-ups.

Healthy Hint

Play games or sports with your family. Tug-of-war is fun! It is a great way to use your muscles.

STRETCHING

Another way to exercise is stretching. It makes our bodies **flexible**. This helps muscles move better. It helps keep us from getting hurt.

MAKE EXERCISE FUN

Walk or ride your bike to school. Or ask a friend to play at the park. These are all ways to exercise. What is your favorite way to exercise?

GET STARTED TODAY

- Exercise for at least 60 minutes every day.

- Play outside instead of watching TV or playing computer games.

- Jump rope to help build strong bones.

- Ride your bike or play tug-of-war to help build strong muscles.

- Plan a family day filled with fun ways to exercise.

- Walk or ride your bike to school.

- Invite a friend to play at the park.

- Get involved in a sport or activity that you like.

WORDS TO KNOW

flexible – able to bend

muscles – tissues in the body that are attached to bones to make them move

oxygen – a gas that humans and animals need to breathe

weight – how heavy a person or an object is

LEARN MORE

Books

Head, Honor. *Keeping Fit*. Mankato, MN: Sea-to-Sea Publications, 2013.

Spilsbury, Louise. *Get Active!* New York: Crabtree Publishing, 2011.

Web Sites

BAM! Body and Mind
http://www.cdc.gov/bam/activity/cards.html
Learn more about different kinds of activities and the gear you need to play.

KidsHealth
http://kidshealth.org/kid/stay_healthy/fit/work_it_out.html
Read more about how exercise keeps us healthy and happy.

PBS Kids
http://pbskids.org/curiousgeorge/games/monkey_moves
/monkey_moves.html
Get up and move with Curious George!

INDEX

bones, 14, 17
breathing, 13

heart, 10

lungs, 13

muscles, 17, 18

oxygen, 10, 13

playing outside, 9
pull-ups, 17
push-ups, 17

riding bike, 5, 21
running, 5, 10

sports, 14, 17
stretching, 18

weight, 6